The Moon Shone Bright

The Moon Shone Bright

a play by
Des Walsh

BREAKWATER

BREAKWATER
100 Water Street
P.O. Box 2188
St. John's, NF
A1C 6E6

National Library of Canada Cataloguing in Publication Data

Walsh, Des
The moon shone bright : a play by Des Walsh.

ISBN 1-55081-195-9
1. Newfoundland and Labrador--History--1949- --Drama.
I. Title.

PS8595.A586M66 2002   C812'.54   C2002-903853-7
PR9199.3.W352M66 2002

Design/Layout: Rhonda Molloy & Carola Kern

ALL RIGHTS RESERVED. No part of this work covered by the copyright hereon may be reproduced or used in any form or by any means—graphic, electronic or mechanical—without the prior written permission of the publisher. Any request for photocopying, recording, taping or storing in an information retrieval system of any part of this book shall be directed in writing to the Canadian Reprography Collective, 6 Adelaide Street East, Suite 900, Toronto, Ontario, M5C 1H6. This applies to classroom usage as well.

The Canada Council | Le Conseil des Arts
for the Arts | du Canada

We acknowledge the financial support of The Canada Council for the Arts for our publishing activities.

 We acknowledge the financial support of the Government of Canada through the Book Publishing Industry Development Program (BPIDP) for our publishing activities.

Printed in Canada.

Production History

The Moon Shone Bright was commissioned by Rising Tide Theatre, Donna Butt, Artistic Director, for the Summer in the Bight Theatre Festival and was first produced in Trinity, Trinity Bay, Newfoundland, in 1999.

Director	Richard Rose
Mary	Ruth Lawrence
Bill	Jerry Doyle
Jack	Ed Kielly
Uncle Peter	Rick Boland
Sarah	Michelle Rex
Leo	Lawrence Barry
Vince	Dennis Hookey

Playwright's Notes

The Moon Shone Bright takes its name from an old English Christmas carol that was collected and continues to be sung in southeastern Trinity Bay, namely the Heart's Delight - Green's Harbour area. The characters in this play are fictitious, the community fictitious. However, some of the events are based on my own family and the stories I grew up hearing as a post-Confederate child. From the original production, I thank Anita Best, Guy Sprung, Don Walsh and Tickle Harbour, Snotty Var, Donna Butt and Rising Tide Theatre and Richard Rose. Finally, I boldly suggest a poem to help set the tone of the piece.

March 3, 1999 - Notes on an upcoming anniversary

We are North Americans now
the same as those Pablo Neruda wearied of,
lulled into the same crimes,
the same culture-starved wanderings.
Fifty years ago we were Europeans,
singing stubbornly into the face of wind
cutting masts for schooners that would sail forever,
cutting pine for the churches of England.
Fifty years ago we were lean and sensual,
our mouths unhurriedly pressed into each other,
our tongues touched whatever God we wanted.
Before our glistening fish, salted for Portugal
and Spain, became the currency of theatre,
before being slaughtered in wars far from
the coves we wandered as children,
we pressed wild berries to our lips
and wiped the pungent juices from our mouths,
the blood red placenta of the promise of a healthy future.
And now, the disease spreading, we weep together,
collectively walking to every graveyard on every headland
and bury men and rodneys, women and knowledge.
We close the lodges and the halls, remove the steeples,
abandon the headstones, haul the doors of the trap, leave rosary beads
between stone and seaweed, leave saw blades to rust behind hills,
half-empty dippers of berries spilling into
the mossy barrens, leave our sensuality circling the tops of
fog-wrapped fir trees. And now, fifty years later,
having done as we're told, we are left to celebrate.

Des Walsh

Hog's Nose, Trinity
Trinity Bay, Newfoundland

List of Characters:

Mary Greene

Bill, her husband

Jack, Bill's brother

Uncle Peter

Sarah, Jack's wife

Leo, Mary and Bill's older son

Vince, their youngest son

ACT I

Scene I

Prologue

Soft lights up on a stage where the set is barely illuminated. It is Christmas Eve, 1948. We hear carol singers somewhere outside in the distance.

CAROL SINGERS *(off stage)*

The moon shines bright and the stars give light
A little before it is day
The moon shines bright and the stars give light
A little before it is day
Our Lord our God he calls on us
And bids us to watch and to pray.

Awake, awake good people all,
Awake and ye shall hear
Awake, awake good people all,
Awake and ye shall hear
Our Lord our God died on the cross
For those whom he loved so dear.

Des Walsh

There's a talent at your head, young man
And another at your feet
There's a talent at your head, young man
And another at your feet
When your good deeds and your bad ones
Together they both shall meet.

The carol singers fade and we hear two voices speaking from an imaginary upstairs room.

MARY *(off stage)*

Do ya find it cold Bill?

BILL *(off stage)*

No...and neither will you if ya just stop talkin' and let me go about me business.

Mary laughs.

MARY *(off stage)*

Good Lord my love...'tis after twelve o'clock...yer after goin' about yer business already. Let's go to sleep now...please...

BILL *(off stage)*

December 24, 1948...our last Christmas as Newfoundlanders Mary, and you wants to go to sleep.

MARY *(off stage)*

Confederation is not gonna stop me puttin' me legs around ya b'y!

BILL *(off stage)*

Are ya sure? 'Cause if I thought it true, I'd go right now and shoot

The Moon Shone Bright

Joe Smallwood and every one of the seventy-eight thousand three hundred and twenty-three that voted for 'im...

MARY *(off stage)*

Go to sleep...

Pause

MARY *(off stage)*

I love you Bill.

Lights out.

Scene 2

Lights up on an outport kitchen, early morning, 1955. Bill is seated at the table when Mary enters. An oil lamp illuminates a table littered with liquor bottles, glasses and food. A daybed is along a wall. A radio on a shelf plays music of the period.

BILL

Are they still asleep?

MARY

Sure ya know now...Vince was tired enough but not Leo...up all night as usual.

Mary begins clearing away.

MARY

It was a grand night all the same, wasn't it?

BILL

It certainly was, sweetheart...

MARY

Are ya sure your Uncle Peter is okay?

BILL

I was worried about the stove, girl...when he fell and struck it, the dampers popped out of the holes for Christ sake.

MARY

Bill!

BILL

I'm sure he's fine, my love, it was his seventieth birthday and he got a bit on the go is all...knocked himself senseless long enough for someone else to sing a song all the same.

MARY

April 22, 1955...can ya believe it?

BILL

Six years as Canadians, Mary...

MARY

How do ya feel?

BILL

Like I was lied to...the Imperial Tobacco Company is gone, the Colonial Cordage Company is gone. They says that the Canadian companies are bringin' in the same things for cheaper 'cause of there's no tariffs on any of it anymore.

MARY

Well that's the one thing that can't be all bad if it come true...that we're s'posed to see a reduced price on stuff. But it won't, you mark my words.

BILL

And they're sayin' now that our own businesses, all them places that makes the stuff we got, will close down before long and all those people will be put out of work.

MARY

'Tis odd the things ya never heed…I heard on the radio the other day that there was one year we made over 280 tons of nails right here in Newfoundland. I never thought about it before, a foolish thing as nails, but now we're bringin' in nails from outside and our foundaries are closin'.

BILL

And that's why I'm glad I'm at what I'm at…there's no one gonna throw me out of me motor boat…there'll always be fish that's one thing for sure…and Newfoundlanders will always be fishin'…there's nothin' Canada can do about that.

MARY

It was good of Uncle Peter not to bring it all up again with Dan Reid, all the same.

BILL

I'm not so sure about all that. I don't think Uncle Peter knows either. But if Dan did vote Confederation six years ago, he voted 'cause of that God damn old age pension…Uncle Peter figured that was the one sure reason why he was God damn ashamed to be in here with the lot of us, when he knew how we all voted in this harbour, and Dan Reid from down the shore.

MARY

At least he wasn't as bad as some of them goin' on about it all the time and crossin' over at the last minute. He was quiet about it, he kept it to himself.

Pause.

The Moon Shone Bright

BILL

Just imagine…those two youngsters we got aren't Newfoundlanders.

MARY

Oh yes they are.

BILL

On paper they're Canadians, Mary…part of the Dominion.

MARY

On paper we're all Canadians, Bill…anyway, enough talk about it. We gotta' get on with what we gotta' do.

BILL

We're gonna be talkin' about it for a long while yet, you mark my words. Losin' yer country by thievery and bribery isn't somethin' that people just roll over and forget about I can tell you that.

Mary and Bill listen to the sounds of the kitchen. Mary looks at her husband teasingly.

MARY

I'm goin' back to bed for an hour…you?

BILL

Are ya askin' me to yer bed there, woman?

MARY

If you'll have me?

Bill stands up and puts his arms around her.

BILL

And that I will you beautiful creature, and that I will…don't you tease me this mornin'…where in the hell is Jack…look at the time!

MARY

When has your brother ever been on time?

The door opens.

JACK

I heard that…that's why I never stomps me boots comin' into the porch in this house 'cause you'll always hear somethin' about yourself if you're quiet.

MARY

Will ya have tea Jack?

BILL

I thought you were goin' back to bed for a spell…we haven't got time for tea!

JACK

I'd love a cup of tea, Mary…and a slice of bread. Grand night last night, me head is like boiled turnip left in a pot for five days.

Mary pours hot water in the teapot.

BILL

What's wrong with tea and bread in your own house b'y?

JACK

Don't taste the same…

MARY

Ya needs a woman.

BILL

He needs a kick in the arse is what he needs.

MARY

Ah stop it Bill...you have another cup yerself.

JACK

Yes b'y...and where were you when me and Uncle Peter were down in the stage to start the stove a good half-hour ago?

MARY

Uncle Peter?

BILL

'Twere you got him up I s'pose!

JACK

He wants to be up, Bill. And I say let 'im. What's he gonna do but sit around my place all day and look out that God damn window out across the harbour. 'Tis killin' 'im not bein' at anything and you knows it yourself!

BILL

He's livin' with you so as to take it easy, not be up at the crack of day to go down into a freezin' fish stage to mend nets! He wouldn't rest here with the youngsters on the go day and night.

JACK

He's livin with me 'cause it'd drive 'im off his head to be livin' with you is all it is. Sweet Christ, Mary, I don't know how ya puts up with 'im.

MARY

It's only out of care for Uncle Peter, Jack…he's gettin' on is all he's sayin'…

JACK

Sure he don't have a worry in the world with the pension rollin' in!

BILL

God damn you this very morning…'tis good poor Mother and Father are cold in the ground…'cause either one of 'em would smack ya across the face if they were here!

MARY

That's enough of it now…

JACK

Ah me and Uncle Peter are rollin' in it right enough! Do you know that on the cheque there's a picture of Joe Smallwood on one side and Louis St. Laurent on the other!

Bill pushes back the chair as he stands abruptly.

MARY

That's enough…not in this house…never again I said!

JACK

Whaddya think, Bill…do ya think you're the only one in the harbour that voted against Confederation. We all voted against it b'y, most of us anyway…but it's done now, the friggin' deed is done.

BILL

'Tis not done then...it'll never be done...not for me...not for her...not for my youngsters, not for my Father and Mother, not for Uncle Peter! It might be done for you and a lot like ya...thinkin' that yer country is gone because some bald, eye-glassed bastard like Joe Smallwood says it is!

Mary takes the teapot and goes to the door and steps outside. She returns.

MARY

Now I knows there's cups down there in the stage so the the two of ye can have yer tea down there. I want both of ye out of this house this minute or I'll let fly the kettle at the two of ye!

Scene 3

Bill and Jack are in the fish stage with their Uncle Peter. All three are mending a cod trap.

JACK

Just got out with our lives I'm tellin' ya.

UNCLE PETER

She was right enough…she shouldn't have warned ye all the same. There's no man should be shoutin' and bawlin' in a woman's kitchen. Your poor Aunt Helen, God rest her, a kitchen's only for eatin' and singin' she'd always say. Men wants to shout and bawl let 'em do it when their out haulin' a trap…that way only the gulls can hear their bullshit and not half what's in the harbour.

JACK

You're all set for tomorrow then…yer still gonna go?

BILL

Don't you worry about me Jack. First light and I'll be well on me way…

JACK

Well b'y you're the one who's hell bent on buyin' it.

BILL

It's a good price for a cod trap…besides, this one is not gonna take too much more mendin'. We need another one and Dan only used the trap one season.

UNCLE PETER

'Tis smellin' like weather all the same.

BILL

Well there's nothin' I can do about it. When I seen 'im last month, tomorrow was the day I told 'im I'd be there with the money. I give 'im my word. I never expected the ice would be in this quick. I gotta' walk and that's all there's to it.

UNCLE PETER

You're good for fifteen mile in good weather, Bill, but there's easterlies comin' all the same. And the way this day is goin', ya can smell it I'm tellin' ya. Every damn dog in the harbour was howlin' last night and that's a sure sign of an easterly wind.

BILL

I'll get there…probably won't be all that bad. I'm only goin' over to pay 'im, it's not like I got to carry it home on me back.

The men continue mending in silence.

JACK

Whaddya make of 'em buildin' a new wharf?

BILL

'Tis all right I s'pose b'y…

JACK

A few jobs puttin' 'er there too.

Uncle Peter's voice rises in agitation.

UNCLE PETER

My Jesus listen to the two of ye...it's workin' that's for God damn sure.

JACK

What?

UNCLE PETER

The horseshit that yer swallowin' from Ottawa.

BILL

What's Ottawa got to do with the wharf?

UNCLE PETER

What in the name of sweet Christ are those wharves called in other harbours that got 'em...that's right, ' the government wharf' is what they're called. And now they're gonna put one here, and who do ya think is the government, us here in the harbour...no my son, that was all decided somewhere up there, by someone other than ourselves.

JACK

What harm can a new wharf do, Uncle Peter?

UNCLE PETER

What was ever wrong with the family stage, you tell me that? Hundreds of years of sweat and fish guts right here where we're sittin'...you listen here, it's a way for them to get us all under one roof where they can keep an eye on us, regulate us as they call it. The only crowd a government wharf helps is the merchant and federal fisheries. You mark my words, doin' away with the family stages and flakes is gonna take the heart out of every harbour in Newfoundland.

All three fall silent while continuing with their work.

BILL

Young Sarah Pinsent is back.

JACK

She's twenty-eight Bill...

UNCLE PETER

She's a lot younger than you right enough...so that must make you an ol' dog then Jack.

BILL

The first Canadian job in the harbour.

JACK

And I'd just as soon see someone from the harbour get it...she been post mistress for six years in...in...ah wherever the Christ she's been this past while.

UNCLE PETER

What happens to the stamps?

BILL

What?

UNCLE PETER

The Newfoundland stamps....Christ Almighty, I got a fortune in stamps. Poor Helen would buy 'em up like they were food stamps from the thirties, and now I got a box of stamps and I don't know if they're any good anymore.

BILL

I never thought about it.

JACK

Sure Sarah will know all about that.

UNCLE PETER

And what about me money?

BILL

What money?

JACK

Ah for Christ sake, Uncle Peter, it's been six years…we knew about that. We were told anyone could take their money to Clarenville and get it turned in…ya haven't still got Newfoundland money!

Uncle Peter bristles.

UNCLE PETER

Turned in for what?

JACK

Canadian money.

UNCLE PETER

What in the hell's flames is wrong with Newfoundland money?

It were good enough for any merchant in any bay in Newfoundland for all these years before…what's wrong with it now? Has it got some God damn disease that if a Canadian touches it, they'll break out in a rash?

BILL

How much have ya got?

UNCLE PETER

I dunno'…'bout three or four hundred dollars I s'pose.

Jack and Bill are amazed.

UNCLE PETER

Get the stund looks off yer faces….I had it put away and your Aunt Helen had some put away too. I was gonna send it in to Peter Cashin and them but then I didn't figure I needed to.

JACK

Why?

UNCLE PETER

'Cause I didn't think we were gonna lose God damn it. I didn't think we'd lose the country.

JACK

No…why send it into them?

BILL

'Cause they needed it ya omagon!

UNCLE PETER

That friggin' lyin' creature Smallwood said there was no money comin' in from Canada during the campaign but there was...everyone knows that now, that Ottawa was bankrollin' the Confederates.

JACK

Give it up Uncle Peter...

UNCLE PETER

What..'tis the truth God damn it!

Jack winks at Bill.

JACK

Truth! Sure maybe we all knows the truth...p'rhaps the whole God damn harbour knows the truth!

BILL

Careful, Jack...

UNCLE PETER

The truth about what?

JACK

Maybe how ya voted your own self...

BILL

Ah for Christ sake.

UNCLE PETER

How I voted...whaddya mean how I voted. What in the name of

Jesus are you on about my son? I voted how any one with any sense voted.

JACK

Ya voted for the pension...tell the truth...there's nothin' wrong with that, a man your age...we understands, don't we, Bill...but just stop the horseshit that's all. 'Tis all right for ya to...

Uncle Peter is up and grabs Jack by the collar and throws him across the room where he lands hard on the floor.

UNCLE PETER

It's only because you're me brother's son that I don't kill ya right here and now!

Uncle Peter leaves as Jack gets to his feet.

BILL

You all right?

JACK

By Christ there's nothin' wrong with the strength in his arms, I can tell ya that!

Scene 4

Mary and Sarah Pinsent are sitting at the kitchen table while Mary unwraps a brown-paper package. A roaring wind is heard from outside as a snow storm rages.

MARY

Well I'll tell ya this much, Sarah, they took their own sweet time gettin' it back out from St. John's....I sent it in almost a year ago.

SARAH

What is it?

MARY

The radio...when Uncle Peter heard the final vote the night of Confederation, he walked over and put his fist down through it, as calm as if he were gettin' a glass of water.

SARAH

They may well have taken their time sendin' it out Mary but you sure as hell took your own time sendin' it in.

MARY

I couldn't afford to get it done before, girl.

Mary removes the still battered radio from the wrapping—it's in pieces.

SARAH

Oh my Lord!

Mary removes a piece of paper from the wreckage.

SARAH

What does it say?

Mary reads from the note.

MARY

'Dear Mrs. Greene…radio returned as received…there was nothing left to repair.'

SARAH

Ah sure they don't make radios like they used to.

MARY

They don't make fists like Uncle Peter's anymore either.

Mary looks anxiously to the window.

SARAH

Sure ya knows he stayed there, Mary.

MARY

Yes, girl, I allow…as foolish as he is at times I dare say he's stayed put somewhere.

SARAH

Never mind Bill now…what about Jack?

MARY

What about 'im?

SARAH

Oh listen to 'er....I knows now you haven't sized up that cute little backside of his when he walks away...

MARY

'Tis his brother's backside I watches, Sarah, and the only one I've watched since I were seventeen.

SARAH

Like they say, Mary...'tis no matter where a woman gets her appetite, so long as she has her dinner at home.

MARY

Stop yer idleness...

SARAH

Is Jack spoken for?

MARY

Not that I know of, girl.

SARAH

What's wrong with 'im tho' I wonder?

MARY

What do ya mean?

SARAH

For him to be on his own with no woman, and he after buildin' a house for himself years ago, why don't a woman have 'im is what I mean!

MARY

Who for God sake...there's not one single woman in the harbour, 'cept for poor Nellie McCarthy, and she don't know the war is over...poor thing with her oars right out of the water since the fairies took 'er...

SARAH

Are ya sure?

MARY

My Lord, Sarah, you knows Nellie as well as I do, she were never right since she were borned...then the fairies took 'er on her tenth birthday, sure they might just as well as took 'er right out of the cradle....

SARAH

No, no...no single woman in the harbour I mean.

MARY

Not one.

SARAH

There is now then....Sarah Pinsent the post mistress, as single as the day she come into the world...what about Chance Cove and Chapel Arm and places like that, any single ones there?

MARY

Sweet Christ, Sarah, I don't know every single woman on this side of the bay ya know!

SARAH

It's just if I goes after 'im I wants to be sure of me chances.

MARY

I'd say now the post mistress with the federal government got a damn site better of a chance than any other…single or no.

SARAH

That government is gonna give me a raise…

MARY

I hope that's not the only reason we give up the country, Sarah, so as you could get a raise…my Bill or Jack or none of the other fishermen are gettin' a raise I can tell you that.

SARAH

That's not my fault, my dear…I'm only here to sort the mail…

MARY

Sort the baby bonus ya mean…

SARAH

I knows you turns yours back in now, Mary. When you gets your cheque every month, whaddya do with it…flick it down on the landwash with the cabbage water do ya?

The door opens and in walks Jack.

JACK

And that's what she don't…she's savin' up to go to St. John's on the train to buy silk stockings to drive me poor brother clear off his head.…

MARY

Listenin' in as always...

SARAH

Do ya like silk stockings, Jack?

JACK

What kind of question is that, Sarah...I likes wool socks, good old wool socks...like any natural man would.

SARAH

On a woman ya foolish creature, do ya like silk stockings on a woman?

Jack is uncomfortable, embarrassed at the talk.

JACK

I dunno'...maybe I do...I ah...

MARY

Tea, Jack?

JACK

Oh God I'd love a cup, Mary...what about a cold glass of water first, 'tis enough to bake ya in here, girl, yer gonna split the top of the stove with the heat.

SARAH

A woman knows how to warm a kitchen, Jack...and other things too isn't that right, Mary?

MARY

A slice of bread, Jack?

JACK

Be God p'rhaps I will...

SARAH

Well if that's one thing I like, is my hands in dough...when it's nice and warm and soft and ya squeezes it and runs right mushy between your fingers...

Jack and Mary are looking at Sarah.

MARY

What are ya makin' Sarah...bread or rice pudding? 'Cause if it's bread, and ya got dough runnin' through your fingers, a goat wouldn't eat it!

The door opens and in comes Uncle Peter.

UNCLE PETER

No sign of 'im?

MARY

Don't you get worried, Uncle Peter...if you're worried I'll get in an awful way.

UNCLE PETER

Well I am worried then. He should have been back by now.

JACK

He's stayin' over...

SARAH

Will I get your tea, Jack?

UNCLE PETER

Well, I'm goin' after 'im if he don't show up soon.

JACK

I knows you are now...

MARY

I'm gonna' go with ya too, Uncle Peter.

SARAH

Do you want your bread toasted on the stove, Jack?

MARY

Will you shut up about the tea and the bread, Sarah!

JACK

By the time he got there, here's what happened...now listen to me...yes the storm came on before he got to Dan Reid's house right enough...

SARAH

It isn't very polite to tell someone to shut up, Mary.

UNCLE PETER

Will ya not listen for a minute, Sarah Pinsent...you're your mother's people make no mistake.

JACK

He paid Dan for the cod trap, they poured themselves a drink, the storm got worse and that's where Bill is right now, planked on his arse next to the stove, with by now, a half a bottle of rum in 'im, as safe as in the arms of Jesus.

Loud stomping of boots is heard from the porch. The door opens and in comes an exhausted Bill.

MARY

My God, look at the state of you...

UNCLE PETER

What in hell's flames were you thinkin' about to walk back in this?

BILL

He sold it.

Sarah goes to the stove.

SARAH

Say what you like Mary...I'm gettin' your husband a cup of tea then, if no one bawls at me for doin' it that is.

JACK

Who sold what?

BILL

The cod trap, God damn it!

MARY

He couldn't have...

BILL

Well he did then…I barely made it to his door, knocked on it, and out he came. I holdin' out the money in me mitt and said I was there to pay 'im for the trap and he told me it was already sold…he sold it last week to a good man he said, a man that voted for Confederation and not against it. I were that mad I struck 'im right where he stood. Then I turned around and headed home.

UNCLE PETER

The bastard…I'll drown 'im. You mark my words. If I sees Dan Reid anywhere near the water I'll drown 'im! Never mind his God damn turncoat soul, he dug his own grave with this!

Bill stands as Uncle Peter storms out.

BILL

I got to go and lie down. If I talks anymore about it I'm as likely to start to bawl in front of the lot of ye.

Bill goes upstairs leaving the others to their own silence.

SARAH

There's nothing wrong with a man crying…nothing at all…do you ever cry Jack?

Scene 5

Bill is sitting off to the side while Mary sits at the kitchen table. An oil lamp is their only light. In the background, a radio plays Country and Western music from the fifties.

BILL

Oh Christ can ya turn that off?

Mary gets up and turns off the radio.

MARY

Sometimes there's a good song comes on…I like that one by Hank Lochlin but he haven't played it tonight.

Pause

BILL

What do ya think, Mary…are we gonna make it or what?

MARY

Sure ya knows we are…we'll be all right. We're tired is all, we've had a long day. Let's go to bed.

BILL

Them two boys are not growin' fast enough. I need 'em both with me in the boat to make a go of it.

MARY

Don't wish your time away, Bill…

BILL

I miss a song...or a good dance.

MARY

We had a song not long ago.

BILL

It's like the few that were at it years ago are embarrassed about it now all the same. With all the stuff comin' in over the radio...it's like they don't want to stand out too much, like they're ashamed of bein' who they are...I don't know what I'm tryin' to say, girl....

Mary laughs.

MARY

Ya don't miss bein' single tonight do ya?

BILL

By God I certainly don't...I miss me Mother singin' is what I miss...my God, she had songs that I wouldn't say Adam and Eve heard, they were that old. And Father, for all he drank...he was always there, always had a way to fix any problem that come to him. And with them both gone, I don't know what it is, girl...I got you I know, and I got the boys...but it was like it all came too quick on the heels of losin' the two of them...I lost me Mother and Father and I lost me country...all before I was twenty-five.

MARY

Do ya want me sing to ya?

BILL

Would ya...just a verse or two?

Des Walsh

Mary sings softly. The song is the Newfoundland version of the traditional ballad 'Jimmy and Nancy'.

MARY

So late so late one evening,
in the lovely month of May
We hoisted our Newfoundland colours,
for Boston sailed away
Where the hills and trees were guarded,
with pretty girls all round
We had one sailor lad on board,
all in his uniform.

He wrote his love a letter,
give her to understand
That he was going to leave her,
all to some foreign land
When she received this letter,
straight way to him did go
Sayin' Jimmy my love Jimmy,
are you going to leave me so.

Mary hums a few notes of the song.

MARY

Bill...?

There is no reply. Bill has fallen asleep in the chair.

MARY

My sweet, sweet man.

❖❖❖

ACT II

Scene 1

It is 1979 and the scene opens in Mary and Bill's kitchen. The furniture has changed, somewhat reflecting the time. The door opens and in comes Leo, a young man in his late twenties. He turns on a radio to the sound of a rock song from the period.

LEO

Mudder!

Leo goes to the fridge and opens it and takes out a log of bologna. He goes to the table and cuts off a slice.

LEO

Mudder! Where the hell are ya, girl?

Leo munches on the raw bologna as his mother comes in the door with a load of laundry.

MARY

What are ya roarin' out about, my son? Turn down that will ya!

LEO

Were ya to the mail...Aunt Sarah have me cheque?

MARY

No I wasn't to the mail...I'm up to me ears with more to do than collect your mail, Leo.

Mary lays down her load of laundry and goes and turns down the radio.

LEO

Where's Dad?

MARY

Down in the stage cuttin' up bait with your brother Vince and Uncle Jack and Uncle Peter...where you should be.

LEO

I'm in the plant mudder, I'm workin'...I don't need to be in the fish stage no more...no more cuttin' friggin' herrin' in chunks for me.

MARY

You're not in the plant then...you're laid off like half what's in the harbour and you're gettin' an unemployment cheque. So don't stand there and tell me you're workin'. People in Newfoundland used to work...

LEO

Oh, Jesus, don't start on that again will ya! You cashed the baby bonus all them years.

MARY

Your Uncle Peter down there don't then...never cashed a pension cheque since 1949. And you wouldn't know but the end of the world is come if that cheque of yours is a day late.

LEO

Where's me blue shirt?

MARY

I've no idea...

LEO

Ah for Christ sake, mudder, I told ya me and the boys were going into St. John's and I needed the blue shirt.

The phone rings. Leo answers it.

LEO

Hello...hey what are ya at, man?...Ya did...no I didn't friggin' get mine...ya lend me forty bucks I guess...who's pickin' us up? Good enough.

Leo hangs up the phone as the door opens and Bill and Vince enter.

BILL

Sweet Christ I'm starved!

Bill goes over and turns off the radio.

VINCE

Me too.

LEO

You're always starved, Vince...every time ya come through the—you friggin' nuisance...that's me blue shirt on ya...who told ya to put it on?

VINCE

Shag off, Leo...it was in me drawer b'y!

LEO

Did you put it in his drawer, mudder?

MARY

I dunno' b'y...

BILL

Will all of ye stop bawlin' like scalded pigs?

LEO

I was gonna wear it to go to town.

Vince takes off his coat and begins undoing the shirt.

VINCE

Here...take the God damn thing ya friggin' arsehole!

LEO

Yes sure now...and the smell of twine and herrin' on it...

BILL

What's wrong with the smell of twine and herrin', my son...not good enough for ya now, is that it.

The door opens and Sarah enters with a brown envelope in her hand.

SARAH

Who's not good enough?

MARY

Nothing, Sarah…

SARAH

I was on my way home to get Jack and Uncle Peter their dinner and thought I'd drop this in to you, Leo.

She hands him the envelope.

LEO

God bless ya Aunt Sarah…can't change it can ya?

SARAH

No…but I've done ya a little favour. I'm closed for dinner. No one else will get a cheque until I open up again so go on down to the shop now and they'll change it for you.

MARY

Are ya havin' a bite to eat before you go, Leo?

LEO

Nah…me and the b'ys will stop at the Irving.

BILL

Yes my son, be sure and give your money to the Irvings now won't ya. Get yer gas there too 'cause you wouldn't wanna' fill 'er up here in the harbour and give a few dollars to poor ol' John Lynch down there now would ya!

LEO

Oh sweet Christ, Father, give it up will ya! I gotta' clear outta' this place and that's all there's to it…

Leo grabs his coat and leaves.

SARAH

I better get over home…

BILL

Yes, girl…ya don't want to be late openin' up the post office on U.I. day or the crowd around here will as likely kick the doors in.

SARAH

It's their money, Bill…they worked for it.

BILL

Yes I know they did a hell of a lot of work…

MARY

That's enough now…we'll see ya later, Sarah.

SARAH

Good enough then.

Sarah leaves.

VINCE

We got to fill out those forms, Dad….

BILL

I can't face on that now, Vince, my son.

VINCE

Well ya got to face on it now...or the fisheries crowd are gonna shut us down if we don't get the licences all straightened up.

MARY

And my form goes in with it don't forget. I'm in the boat next season and that's all there's to it, not another word about it.

BILL

Forms, letters, fees...Christ Almighty, every God damn thing Peter Cashin said before '49 is true...there's no one will ever know how much I hate everything west of Port aux Basques and what's happened to this place....

VINCE

Oh, if they lived with ya they might have an idea, Dad...where's the forms, Mom?

Scene 2

Lights up on the kitchen where Bill, Mary, an aging Uncle Peter, Jack and Sarah are in the middle of a game of cards called 'Auction'....Sarah is dealing. Leo is sitting off by himself reading an auto magazine.

JACK

Give us some cards this time, Sarah...I haven't made a bet in five hands.

SARAH

What's the score?

MARY

No one there yet, girl...Bill is the most...he's thirty-five.

UNCLE PETER

Who's thirty-five?

MARY

Bill...

UNCLE PETER

You'll never see thirty-five again my son...

JACK

His score is thirty-five, Uncle Peter,...not his age.

LEO

Look at this, Uncle Jack...a '66 Mustang...

BILL

Twenty...

MARY

Pass me...

LEO

I'd say she'd do me...

JACK

'66 Mustang...she'd do ya right enough...

BILL

Twenty to you Jack.

JACK

What did you say, Mary?

BILL

She passed b'y...

UNCLE PETER

Twenty-five...

BILL

Hang on, Uncle Peter...Jack's bid.

Des Walsh

JACK

Pass...

UNCLE PETER

Twenty-five...

SARAH

Go on...

UNCLE PETER

Clubs...

The players discard while Sarah gives them second cards.

BILL

Get me another beer there will ya, Leo.

Leo goes to the fridge and peers in.

LEO

All the Jockey are gone...gonna have to be a Molson Canadian, Dad.

BILL

I'll perish from thirst first...get me a rum and water...the bottle is there under the sink.

Leo does as told.

JACK

I'll have a Canadian then when ya gets a chance, Leo.

SARAH

It's a good beer, isn't it?

BILL

Moose piss is all it is.

UNCLE PETER

Callin' for the ace of clubs...

MARY

Oh Lord, Uncle Peter got 'em this time...

The door opens and Vince comes in.

MARY

Where were you, honey?

VINCE

Down the harbour puttin' an arse in a rodney.

MARY

Your supper is in the oven...probably ruined now.

LEO

Whose rodney?

VINCE

Clarence's...

The card players continue laying their cards in succession, the winner gathering in the pile as the hands are played.

LEO

Clarence who?

VINCE

Clarence Pinsent b'y...

LEO

What does Clarence Pinsent want to put a rodney back in the water for?

VINCE

He wants to put his cow back on the island and the damn thing is afraid of the motor boat, so he'll skull 'er back and forth in the rodney.

LEO

Why don't he just shoot the God damn ol' cow?

VINCE

It's one of the last cows in the harbour, Leo...he wants to keep 'er I s'pose.

LEO

The last rodney too...

UNCLE PETER

And it'll soon be the last fish.

LEO

No way...there's plenty of fish.

UNCLE PETER

Ya knows no more than the wood box, Leo.

SARAH

Who's run in?

JACK

Yours isn't it, Bill?

The players continue their card laying in turn.

LEO

There's tons of fish I'm tellin' ya...I sees it at the plant.

BILL

How come you're shut down if there's tons of fish?

UNCLE PETER

'Cause that crowd are soon gettin' ready to pull out...

VINCE

What did they pay for the plant in the first place...one dollar, wasn't it?

LEO

They put a lot of money into that plant, Vince...and put a lot of people back to work because of it.

UNCLE PETER

The people were never out of work to start with, my son...there was always plenty of work.

Des Walsh

The hand is finished and another deal is supposed to happen, but it doesn't.

SARAH

It's not everyone wants to fish, Uncle Peter...

MARY

I do then when I get my licence...

SARAH

You'll be the talk all this side of the bay, Mary, but I s'pose that's all ya wants is it?

MARY

What I wants, Sarah, is enough money in the house to feed this family.

SARAH

A woman out with her husband in a boat. I never thought I'd see the day.

BILL

God damn it all, Sarah, it'll be soon rare enough to see a man on the water, let alone a woman.

JACK

Whose friggin' deal? Are we playin' cards or what?

UNCLE PETER

Every man on this whole side of the bay is sayin' the same thing...the fish are not there. Ottawa is after licensin' too many draggers I'm tellin' ya, foreign and Canadian.

Another round of cards is dealt.

JACK

There's been lots of years when the fish were not there....1949 for Christ sake was the worst one in years.

UNCLE PETER

It's different I'm tellin' ya...

MARY

Your deal, Bill...

UNCLE PETER

There's somethin' not right out in that bay, the same as most bays around the island and on the Labrador, you mark my words. The Canadian government is about as evil as the Communists, only more sly. More like someone who would walk up behind ya and push ya off the wharf in the middle of winter. Watch ya in the water while the cold makes ya go numb and ya slowly sink below the surface.

SARAH

My God, Uncle Peter...give it up will ya...I got cold shivers all up and down me.

Uncle Peter looks at his cards, bangs hard on the table and shouts loudly.

UNCLE PETER

Thirty for sixty!

Everyone in the room jumps.

Scene 3

Mary and Sarah are sitting at the kitchen table.

MARY

Well, I know this much...every time I turn around to pay for anything it creeps up a little more and a little more...every time there's a budget, the taxes go up.

SARAH

But sure it was no different before, Mary...Mother and Father still paid taxes and the cost of food and clothes were expensive then compared to how much money they had.

MARY

They're goin' about a different way. Bill had a few barrels of fuel come there the week and the price was up by about eleven dollars. We need to get a motor for the boat, and the one we had an eye on the fella' wants eight hundred dollars for 'er, so now we're put off gettin' it.

SARAH

Yes, Jack was sayin'.

MARY

Bill went foolish but the fella' told him they were federal taxes...hidden taxes he called them! They said things would be better but they're worse....

SARAH

But there's nothin' we can do about it, Mary.

MARY

I don't know how you and Jack have done it all these years. I s'pose with you at the post office is what it is, but sure we got Vince with us all the time in the boat and Leo don't cost us anything, but we still finds it hard.

SARAH

You got to watch every cent...

MARY

Christ, Sarah, stop talkin' at me like I was a youngster will ya...

SARAH

You're fifty-three, Mary, hardly a youngster.

MARY

Yes and I'm after forgettin' how to make soap.

SARAH

What foolishness...so what, ya can get soap anywhere and I know you can afford a cake of soap.

MARY

That's not the point...we're all gettin' lazy, the whole place. Christ, Leo works enough when he's on at the plant but soon as he gets the U.I. that's it...lies around like a cut dog.

SARAH

You give all this stuff too much thought, Mary.

MARY

And you don't give it enough!

SARAH

It's 1979, it'll be thirty years next month...thirty years of Confederation, Smallwood is gone, out of politics and half the crowd I know still can't get it out of their God damn veins. Don't you sit there and tell me I haven't thought about it 'cause I have...and I know that it was still the best thing to happen to this place and if you says I think that only because I got a job, I'll smack the face off ya right here in your own kitchen!

MARY

Nice to see there's life in ya...

SARAH

I'm sick of it...I hears it from Uncle Peter from dawn 'till dark.

MARY

I'll be sure to tell 'im ya said that.

Scene 4

Bill, Jack, Uncle Peter and Vince are baiting hooks in the stage while Leo sits nearby.

VINCE

What are ya gonna do, Leo?

LEO

Try for the rigs I s'pose b'y.

BILL

That's no place for a man I can tell ya that right now.

LEO

That's what ya said about the plant.

BILL

The plant is another matter…a twenty-foot sea could do you no harm in a fish plant.

LEO

She's unsinkable, Dad…the new one they're bringin' in.

UNCLE PETER

Royalties for Newfoundland…that's the biggest load of bullshit yet.

JACK

How so?

UNCLE PETER

Do you know anything about the Terms of Union with Canada, Jack? Any dollar we gets from the offshore goes right back to 'em.

JACK

No it doesn't.

UNCLE PETER

Where does it go then?

LEO

Same as Alberta...with their gas and stuff.

UNCLE PETER

You're wrong, my son. I wish ya weren't but you're wrong.

BILL

We never asked for none of this...we were stuck out here in the middle of the Atlantic and wanted to be left alone...no one hardly knew we were here...

UNCLE PETER

Until they wanted us to go over and get our heads, legs and arms blown off in two wars....

LEO

Things are a bit tough now that's all....

VINCE

Tough is not the word, Leo...there's not enough out there for bait.

BILL

The change is too much, too fast…it's all too fast.

LEO

Change…there's no change around here for Christ sake…not in this fish stage anyway…when was the last big change in Newfoundland that anyone can remember?

UNCLE PETER

There were two changes, my son, one was when Captain William Whitely came up with the design for the cod trap back around 1870 and the other was Confederation in 1949!

JACK

That's enough of that…go up to the shop and get a box of beer, Leo…tell 'em to mark it down for me.

BILL

How much beer do ya mark down at all, Jack…where do ya get the money to pay for it is what I'd like to know?

LEO

What kind, Uncle Jack?

JACK

A dozen Canadian…

Leo turns to leave.

JACK

Hold on now…get half a dozen Canadian and half a dozen Jockey, I s'pose. Otherwise the long faces on this crowd will spoil the fish.

Des Walsh

Leo leaves.

UNCLE PETER

I pities the poor young fella', I really do. He's all in a tangle.

VINCE

He's been like that since he was born, Uncle Peter.

UNCLE PETER

Be civil you.

BILL

I done everything I could. There's a place here for 'im with us but he don't want it.

JACK

What...and have you squawkin' at 'im all the time.

BILL

Kiss me arse, Jack...ya knows nothin' about it.

JACK

Yes b'y and you're the expert on it all.

BILL

Ya got no youngsters Jack...never had...never will. So there's one thing I can say I knows more about than you do. And I'll tell you another thing, there's not a young man or woman under twenty-five in Newfoundland who has any idea of what they're doin' anymore. Sweet Christ, you knows yourself, it were only a time ago a man twenty-five would be set if he could manage a full days work.

The Moon Shone Bright

Now be Jesus it's like none of 'em can move off their arse to make a decision for themselves unless the government or some God damn oil company does it for them. Everyone else is makin' decisions for Newfoundlanders is what I'm sayin'!

Scene 5

Late at night, Leo and Vince are sitting at the kitchen table.

LEO

I can show ya me bank book, my son.

VINCE

Does everyone make that much?

LEO

I'm the lowest paid for Christ sake.

VINCE

I dunno', Leo...I don't think I'm right for it. I been on a boat all me life but a rig is another thing altogether.

LEO

You're cracked is what it is. I can get ya on I'm sure of it. And as far as the rig is concerned, it's like sittin' in your own house. And the grub...anything ya want any time of the day.

VINCE

Nah b'y...I think I'll stay here with Mother and Father, in a kitchen I knows is me own. I don't like what I've heard.

LEO

What you've heard is bullshit. There's no need of wastin' everybody's time with all that safety shit. It's Mobil Oil for Christ sake, they know what they're doin', they're doin' it all over the world.

VINCE

Not off the Grand Banks of Newfoundland they haven't.

LEO

The Canadian government regulates them sure.

VINCE

By Christ you've picked out your coffin for sure 'cause the Canadian government don't give a shit about Newfoundlanders on that rig, never have...never will. It was a way to get a few jobs for Newfoundlanders to shut them up while they take all the big money and stuff their pockets so they can build new airports in Toronto and Montreal.

LEO

Do you have any idea how much you sound like Dad and Uncle Peter? How much you're not only thinkin' like 'em but even soundin' like 'em?

VINCE

There's worse people to sound like, Leo.

Vince gets up.

VINCE

I'm goin' to bed.

Leo stands up and follows his brother.

Des Walsh

LEO

'Tis time for you to smarten up my son, and see the writin' on the wall. The harbour is gone my son, it's over, Vince.

They leave the stage.

VINCE *(off stage)*

Listen here, Leo, if you gets up in that room and keeps on, I'm gonna drive me sock down yer throat, do ya hear me!

Lights down.

Scene 6

Lights up on Bill and Mary sitting at the kitchen table.

BILL

Is that the two of them still talkin' up there?

MARY

Yes and don't you dare go up and butt in.

BILL

Vince gotta' get up in the mornin'...'tis all right for Leo.

MARY

Leo is gettin' up too...he's goin' out to the trap with Vince and Jack.

BILL

Well, I don't believe it.

MARY

And don't you make a deal of it.

BILL

How come he won't come out with me and you?

MARY

I think he's still a bit embarassed by it.

BILL

That his mother goes out fishin'.

MARY

Don't say anything to 'im, Bill.

BILL

I won't, girl...I'm tickled to death to have 'im home for a while, the big rig worker with an apartment in St. John's.

MARY

He bought a new television too.

BILL

He told me, and I told him it were a waste of money.

MARY

Well, we gotta' go in next week and sign everything and I'd just as soon have a good place to lie around after that.

BILL

Not gettin' worried about it are ya?

MARY

It's a lot of money to owe, Bill.

BILL

There's no choice...the four of us can crew the one boat instead of runnin' the two we're runnin' now. We gotta' go farther off to get any fish, and the bank and the fisheries department have dangled the carrot. We either get a bigger boat or go on welfare.

MARY

The payments are so damn high all the same...we're gonna have to turn over some fish.

BILL

I'm thinkin' about a crab licence.

MARY

I got more chance of seein' you vote again, Bill, than us gettin' a crab licence...we don't know the right people and you knows just as well as I do that's the way the fisheries works. You vote the right way in an election and the member will see to it that your application doesn't sit on someone's desk...

BILL

And I'm damn well not gonna vote either...they put Responsible Government back on the ballot and I'll vote.

A noise is heard offstage...a voice shouts.

JACK *(off stage)*

Bill! Bill...quick!

BILL *(calling out)*

Christ what is it b'y?

JACK *(off stage)*

Uncle Peter...!

Scene 7

Lights up on Bill and Mary's kitchen where the family sits around the kitchen table. Uncle Peter lies in a coffin off to one side.

BILL

Well that's it then. The Canadian government can finally stop sending Uncle Peter his old age pension cheques. He don't have to send 'em back anymore.

SARAH

The harbour will have nothin' to talk about.

A voice comes from the coffin.

UNCLE PETER

Oh they'll have enough to talk about without me.

No one hears Uncle Peter's voice.

VINCE

I think he finished off the last of his stamps too. What a character. Wouldn't use a Canadian stamp. All them years and he putting Newfoundland stamps on things to send off.

MARY

Well that's it see, 'cause you can put anything on a bill you're payin'. They knows 'tis a payment by the look of the envelope…Marg Ryan never put a stamp on a bill in her life, right, Sarah?

SARAH

As far as I know she hasn't.

JACK

He was a grand hand at the cards...

LEO

I hope he's remembered for more than his card playin'.

Uncle Peter sits up in the coffin.

UNCLE PETER

You listen here, young Leo Greene, there was never such a thing as too much credit given to a good card player. Newfoundland was never hurt by a game of cards.

SARAH

I don't know how ya can sleep in the house all the same, Mary...with a body laid out in your kitchen I mean.

MARY

'Tis only Uncle Peter, Sarah...

BILL

There was no way I was gonna see that man put in a funeral parlour...no one to stay up with 'em.

JACK

Gotta' do everything the old way haven't ya, Bill.

BILL

I'm tryin' to do things the right way that's all.

JACK

Are ya sayin' I don't 'cause I wouldn't lay 'em out in me own house, is that it.

MARY

That's not what anybody is sayin', Jack.

SARAH

Me and Jack would've paid to have him waked in the funeral home.

Uncle Peter climbs out of the coffin.

UNCLE PETER

Yes and ya both could God damn well afford it too!

BILL

Funeral home...home! Why do they call it a home. This is a home.

SARAH

I couldn't do it I'm tellin' ya...I couldn't sleep in a house with a dead body, not for all the money in the world.

UNCLE PETER

Ya don't need all the money in the world, Sarah, ya got enough to do ya...

BILL

Well, it's not like ya don't have the room...a new piece put on yer house...a big new kitchen.

UNCLE PETER

Tell 'em how ya paid for it, Sarah... oh Jesus, Mary, if I could only talk to ya...

JACK

I'm careful with me money...I had some put away.

MARY

No more careful than me and Bill...

LEO

Oh this is good...

VINCE

That's enough out of everyone now...let's not start shoutin' and bawlin' at one another with poor Uncle Peter there in the box.

UNCLE PETER

Oh 'tis all right, Vince, my son, I'm up now anyway. Let 'em all go at it I'd say.

LEO

What about Dan Reid, Uncle Jack?

JACK

What about him?

LEO

Can anyone tell me now, anyone of ye...now that Uncle Peter is gone...did he kill 'im or not?

Des Walsh

The adults are uncomfortable and look at one another for a sign of advice.

UNCLE PETER

Of course I didn't kill 'im…I wanted to all the same.

BILL

That's not for anyone to talk about now, my son.

LEO

Well I heard he did…up to the club last night it were said that Uncle Peter got away with murder.

MARY

Uncle Peter didn't have it in 'im to kill no one…the ice was thin…Dan Reid should've had more sense than be goin' across the arm that time of the year with a horse and a load of wood.

UNCLE PETER

God bless ya, Mary…I always thought the world of ya.

LEO

Uncle Peter was out that day too all the same…how come he got in out of it all right?

Bill's voice rises.

BILL

'Cause he was a smart man is all…he knew ice and he knew water…yes he was out that day, he was cuttin' across the inside of the harbour, but he had sense enough to know where the bad ice was…it were your Uncle Peter who hauled his body across a half a mile of ice for Christ sake!

The Moon Shone Bright

UNCLE PETER

I called out to 'im before he went in...I seen the colour of the ice where he was headin' toward. To this day I wondered if I called out loud enough. Then there's times I figures that's what made the horse veer around was my bawlin'...the slide swung around behind the horse and the next thing there goes Dan and the slide through the ice. P'rhaps I did kill 'im...by bawlin' out I spooked the horse, but by Jesus I'll tell ya this, I wanted to kill that man with me bare hands for sellin' that trap, after Bill there walkin' all that ways on the worst day anyone seen in years, and then sayin' what he said to ya Bill, but I never wanted to see 'im go like that. All I could see was his face as I was tryin' to inch closer to 'im and the horse kickin' me...Dan slidin' in under the water and the pieces of ice cuttin' into his face like glass. I didn't care about Confederation then I can tell ya that or how Dan Reid or anyone else voted. I took a stray piece of wood and started bangin' holes in the ice. I could see him, see...see his face underneath me feet starin' up at me and he wasn't singin' O Canada then I can tell ya that...and I wasn't singin' the Ode to Newfoundland...there was just the three of us out in the middle of the arm that day, two Newfoundlanders and a horse with a load of wood on the ice....

MARY

The saddest part of it all is that he seen the end of it before he left us.

SARAH

The end of what?

MARY

The end of this place as he knew it....

VINCE

We're still here, Mom…we're not goin' anywhere.

LEO

What's that mean, Vince? I'm no good 'cause I'm not still here in the harbour is that it?

BILL

That's not what he's sayin' at all, Leo…

JACK

You done the right thing by gettin' out, my son.

SARAH

That's right, sweetheart…there's nothin' for ya here.

MARY

There's lots here, Sarah…if Leo wants to do something else and work somewhere else that's fine as long as he's happy with it…but don't you sit there and tell me there's nothin' in this harbour or any other place like it in Newfoundland…there's lots here, I'm tellin' ya…

UNCLE PETER

That's the stuff, Mary…give it to 'er!

BILL

The problem is you and people like ya, Sarah, sayin' there's nothin' here…the teachers are tellin' 'em that in school for Christ sake!

SARAH

The young people are all gettin' out and you crowd are so stuck in the God damn past ya can't see the rights of it…

BILL

She's not talkin' about a past, Sarah, she's talkin' about a future....

VINCE

And if everybody believes there's no use in stayin' then they'll all go for sure....

LEO

Lord Jesus, Vince, speak your own mind b'y and not someone else's...

JACK

He can't my son...he's brainwashed by his Mother and Father.

UNCLE PETER

Shut up, Jack!

BILL

Brainwashed is he?

JACK

Yes he is...brainwashed by a fool. 'Tis only 'cause ya can't get over the past like Sarah says.

BILL

And why are you still here, Jack?

JACK

'Cause I knows ya can still make a livin' in the fishery is why...if ya works hard at it.

MARY

And you do work hard at it Jack...all of us have been at it side by side since we were youngsters...and I'd trust you and Sarah with me life, but I got to get this off my chest.

JACK

Get what off yer chest? What are ya talkin' about?

MARY

Remember when Molly Pike hauled me off outside after she come and said her prayers over Uncle Peter...well she whispers to me that Uncle Peter's money were never sent back.

SARAH

Uncle Peter had no money...me and Jack looked out to him. What money are ya talkin' about, Mary?

MARY

Uncle Peter's Canada pension cheques...that's what I'm talkin' about!

UNCLE PETER

O sweet Jesus, someone knew...here we go then...

BILL

Whaddya mean Mary?

MARY

Oh, I'm in an awful way about it, 'cause I know in my heart it can't be true, but she put in my head the only way to know for sure is to call Ottawa and they'd tell us for sure.

The Moon Shone Bright

SARAH

You better know what you're sayin'! Do you hear what you're accusin' your own family of!

MARY

I know it's terrible, Sarah, but it's the only way to put a stop to the talk. If not, the whole harbour will whisper about us for the rest of our days!

SARAH

You're more foolish than I thought, Mary, 'tis the fairies took you is what it is, not poor ol' Nellie McCarthy.

JACK

There's not a word of truth in what Molly Pike is sayin' Mary…it's all horseshit…Uncle Peter give 'em to Sarah every time…she took 'em and sent 'em back every month….

Sarah shifts uncomfortably in her seat.

MARY

Well let's just call then. Let me just go over and pick up the phone and call 'em. If I'm wrong, then I'll be made a fool of, but let me do it right here and now in front of the family. But someone has to do it, Jack, so that the rumour can be put to rest for good.

Jack gets up quickly.

JACK

God damn the lot of ye, I will then! Where's the friggin' phone book. I'll put a stop to this horseshit this minute.

Des Walsh

Sarah cries.

JACK

She always sent 'em back...look what you crowd got done to her now!

BILL

All these years I wonderin' how you two got along as well as ye did....new furniture, big fancy gas barbecue...but by Christ, I never took ya for a thief!

JACK

You God damn bastard...Sarah got raises over the years and always had steady income and she were always good with money. What we did with it is no concern of yours! Now where is the God damn phone book!

Sarah breaks down.

MARY

It's okay, Sarah. It's better to come out with it. It's done now. I just wants to hear ya admit to it.

The room looks on in silent amazement.

SARAH

I did it to help us pay for things...to help us pay for keepin' Uncle Peter with us...I was goin' to stop, then I couldn't...it was so easy to do...Jack knew nothin' about it I swear...I'm sorry, Jack.

BILL

Ya had some nerve to be at it.

JACK

Ya friggin' nuisance...!

SARAH

I didn't keep it all for ourselves...

JACK

Don't say ourselves do ya hear me...I had nothin' to do with it!

UNCLE PETER

I'm sorry too Jack b'y...

SARAH

When Leo had to do the course that time...tell 'em, Leo.

VINCE

That was his own money...he saved it from workin' at the plant.

SARAH

Please, Leo...

LEO

No...I never had enough. Aunt Sarah gave it to me all right. I never knew where it come from tho'.

SARAH

And you, Vince...when I told ya I put your name in that time in that contest and that ya won but not to tell your Mother and Father. There was no contest. I made it up so I could give ya money to go to St. John's when you were chasin' after that young one from

Placentia goin' to school in there....and tell 'em all about the tickets, Jack, I got enough for tickets for all of us to go to Toronto on a trip...

JACK

To hell's flames with Toronto do ya hear me! It don't matter God damn it...ya stole that man's money. The man lyin' there in that coffin...ya stole from 'im!

SARAH

And tell 'em about the motor, Bill...please!

BILL

Tell 'em about what motor, don't haul me into yer thievery.

SARAH

That's how I loaned ya the money that time to pay for the motor, when you and Mary were hard up.

BILL

That's between you and me, God damn it! I paid ya back every cent over the years and now yer throwin' it up in me face in front of me wife and children!

UNCLE PETER

It's all right, Bill, my son...there's no harm now.

Sarah cries.

SARAH

But you knew...I remembers tellin' ya where the money came from in the first place. I know I did.

BILL

Oh Jesus Christ, listen to 'er. 'Tis all bad enough that everyone has to know that I borrowed money from ya but now yer soul is turnin' black with lies.

JACK

He's me brother, Sarah, there's more to 'im than that!

MARY

Leave it now, Jack…it'll never be talked about no more.

JACK

Oh, I'll leave it all right...

Jack storms out of the house.

LEO

Oh Jesus don't cry, Aunt Sarah...

UNCLE PETER

I blame you, Joe Smallwood…yer still shaggin' up this family after all these years. And I won't run into ya because I knows yer in the bowels of hell right enough. 'Less of course God grants me one more wish before he takes me in and I gets me hands around yer damn throat before I sleeps.

ACT III

Scene 1

It is 1999 and Vince, now in his late forties, is sitting at the kitchen table when the door opens and Leo walks in, carrying a suitcase.

VINCE

Well sweet merciful Christ, I don't believe it!

LEO

How are ya, Vince?

VINCE

B'y 'tis not for me to say. It's how are you is the question.

LEO

Pretty good b'y…

VINCE

Not a word from ya that you were comin' home.

LEO

By God now, home…that got a nice sound to it.

VINCE

Where are ya to…last time we heard from ya you were in…where was it…Manitawoudge…with Noranda Mining Company…

LEO

I'm still with Noranda but I'm in Quebec now…I was laid off for a while then hooked a job in Quebec.

VINCE

Still in a mine…

LEO

Still in a mine…

VINCE

How is ah… Susan, is it…and the two youngsters?

LEO

She's fine b'y, and the kids too. They're over in Long Harbour with 'er mother. Christ, I go away and I meet and marry someone a gunshot from where I grew up.

VINCE

How long since ya been home, Leo…not since Uncle Jack died I s'pose, was it…Christ, that's almost ten years now.

LEO

It's been a while hasn't it?

Pause

LEO

I went down to the stage first, just to have a look around but I heard Father and Mother in there and I couldn't handle it…couldn't go in.

VINCE

They're always down there b'y and the two of 'em in their seventies…I'm after givin' up bawlin' at the two of 'em to go up out of it but what harm, I s'pose, they still got to do it their way and I'm the only one still at it, but you knows yourself if I does anything me own way it's not good enough.

LEO

Who's still at it in the harbour?

VINCE

Me…that's it…can ya believe it? I'm the only boat afloat in the harbour. The year of our Lord 1999 and I'm the only man fishin'.

LEO

Still makin' a go of it tho'….

VINCE

I'm makin' a livin' b'y believe it or not. Crab, lobster, lump fish…anything other than cod they'll give me a licence for….

LEO

Any cod out there?

VINCE

There is b'y…up here in this part of the bay there is and all up through the sound, good size fish too but they says they're only bay fish and there's nothin' outside.

Pause

LEO

How are they doin'?

VINCE

Mom is pretty good but Father still got the heart condition as ya know, and I s'pose seein' that's how Uncle Jack and Uncle Peter went, he don't expect to last long, but he's a tough old gad for all that. Jeez, he and mother and Aunt Sarah picked more berries last fall than I seen in me lifetime.

LEO

What about Aunt Sarah?

VINCE

She's not bad…a bit lonely in the house by herself since Uncle Jack died but she's back and forth here all the time.

Both brothers are quiet.

LEO

Ya never took it to get married, Vince.

VINCE

No b'y, I didn't…I seen too much heartache with it…although Mother and Father seem to have worked through it all…you too, I hope.

LEO

I s'pose we have b'y…

Des Walsh

VINCE

How long are ya home for?

Pause

LEO

Tell ya the truth, Vince b'y, I got laid off again…I got hired back about four weeks ago and then laid off again, woke up there on…what's today…Thursday…woke up on Saturday and decided to hell with it…come home for a visit.

VINCE

Yes b'y…just like that…so what are ya gonna do now?

LEO

Tell ya the truth, I'm not sure…not sure at all. Go back out and look for more work I s'pose.

The door opens and in walk Mary and Bill with the ghosts of Uncle Peter and Jack following close behind.

MARY

Oh sweet mother of God!

Leo stands as his mother comes over and throws her arms around him.

BILL

By God, look at yourself.

Leo puts his hand out for the cordial shake but his father embraces him.

UNCLE PETER

Now Jack there ya go see…that's what it is to have youngsters.

JACK

It's all right when they're growed up and sensible, Uncle Peter, no mistake…I would've had youngsters if someone would've passed them over to me when they were thirty and had a job.

UNCLE PETER

Sssshhh…I can't hear what they're sayin!

MARY

How come you're home? What's wrong?

LEO

I'm here for me supper, Mother…

VINCE

Yes and I'm starved to death.

MARY

And I gotta' get more vegetables on…call your Aunt Sarah, Vince, and tell 'er to come up for supper, that Leo is home.

JACK

If you think for one minute that woman don't know Leo is home and…

The door opens and in walks Sarah.

SARAH

No need to call me and I'd love to have supper…come here, Leo, 'til I gets a hold of ya!

Sarah hugs her nephew.

Scene 2

The family are all seated around the table finishing off their supper. The ghosts of Uncle Peter and Jack are off to the side.

LEO

That was perfect....

BILL

They're last years' potatoes too my son...can't beat seaweed and caplin on a garden...

JACK

Here comes the fertilizer line...

BILL

I can taste the fertilizer on store-bought vegetables...

UNCLE PETER

He's right, God damn it...why Newfoundlanders stopped growin' their own vegetables will always be a mystery to me.

SARAH

What's your plans, Leo?

LEO

Lots of plans, Aunt Sarah.

BILL

Yes I know you got lots of plans…how can ya plan up there, my son, when yer gettin' laid off just when ya settles in?

MARY

Why don't ya stay home, honey?

LEO

And do what…?

BILL

There's lots to do, my son…ask Vince here.

LEO

There's not a soul left in the harbour, Dad.

UNCLE PETER

We're still here, Leo my son.

VINCE

Don't start on the harbour, Leo…you're not back a full day…don't start shittin' on the place.

JACK

Oh Christ, don't the two of ye start at it.

MARY

They're gonna lift the moratorium soon, Leo….

BILL

They could lift the God damn thing now!

UNCLE PETER

Give it another year, Bill, don't be too quick with it.

JACK

Sure what good will it do? They'll only lift it and let FPI and National Sea and every foreign trawler out there back on the water again and we'll be right back where we started.

SARAH

Poor old Jack…it would've killed 'im anyway if he had been alive when that got announced.

JACK

What killed me Sarah was all them years of pot liquor…'drink it up my son, the best part of the meal is in the liquor…'

UNCLE PETER

Bullshit…

JACK

What…that's what the doctors all says.

UNCLE PETER

Like old Mr. Clark up in Random Island said…there were no cholesterol around here 'til they put that hospital up in Clarenville! Not workin' is what makes people's hearts give out…once I stopped rowin' a dory, once I got an oil stove put in and stopped cleavin' wood, once I stopped walkin' everywhere and got in a car, once I…

JACK

All right, Uncle Peter, I hear ya b'y…

The Moon Shone Bright

MARY

No more rigs whatever ya do…I'll never forget that night as long as I live…we thinkin' you were on the Ranger the night she went down…that morning listening to the radio, ya remember, Bill?

BILL

Remember it too well and you nuisance ya…on the bender in St. John's and missed your shift but never thought to call out and tell us 'til the middle of the day.

MARY

Funny now thinkin' back on it, how giddy I was with the joy of hearin' your voice and knowin' you were all right and then when I got off the phone it hit me that all them other mothers were gonna get a different kind of call. It broke my heart is what it did and I bawled all day and night…

Mary looks at Bill.

MARY

And you bawled too, Bill…ya wept like a youngster ya did.

UNCLE PETER

We all did, Mary…every Newfoundlander did and I blame Ottawa and the oil companies to this day for every one of them lives lost.

SARAH

That's enough of that now…what about yer woman, Leo? How's yer woman?

BILL

I don't know about the woman part but there's never enough talk of what's right and wrong and the God damn Canadian government has been wrong for fifty years!

JACK

Oh Jesus, here we go…

LEO

Everyone else is wrong is that it…there was never a Newfoundlander wrong…I hear 'em every now and again on CBC being interviewed…blame everyone else.

VINCE

That's not what he's sayin', Leo…and don't talk to me about CBC…the only thing they're interested in is pronouncin' the name of the place proper.

BILL

I'm not too old to speak for me own self, Vince. I can defend it. Sure there was lots Newfoundlanders wrong, me included. Your Uncle Peter was wrong in sendin' back his pension cheque…

JACK

Tryin' to send it back ya mean, Bill…

UNCLE PETER

Sssshhh…

BILL

He should've kept it and spent it and all them years I cursed the unemployment insurance racket and how I used to give you a hard time about it, I was wrong in that. If that God damn crowd are gonna shut rural Newfoundland down and bring it to its knees well by Christ they should pay for it! But that was then and this is now…they set themselves up to be saviours and now they're washin' their hands of us…they're after cuttin' all the fishermen off TAGS and there's no work to get any stamps to get unemployment so the only thing left for Newfoundlanders is to go on the God damn dole, like they were in the thirties and I gotta' sit around here and listen to the likes of Jean Chretien or Brian Tobin or John Crosbie and anyone that came before 'em tell me how good that God damn country of theirs has been to Newfoundland!

UNCLE PETER

By God he's fired up tonight…Bill should've been a politician…missed his callin' he did!

LEO

You're right…

BILL

What…?

LEO

Everything you said…you're right. But so what, no one cares but your own self!

JACK

Christ somethin's about to give…Bill is gonna be here with us if this keeps up.

MARY

Don't be teasin' your father, Leo.

LEO

The problem is that we're a crowd of sheep. We never stood for ourselves.

VINCE

When did you come to this, Leo? Two miles down a mine shaft?

LEO

My question is this, here's Canada, the worst thing to come along says yourself, and we jumped on!

MARY

Not all of us, Leo.

LEO

No, not all of ye but whatever happened, me and Vince here had no say in it.

BILL

Are ya blamin' me and what come before me is that it?

LEO

I'm blamin' all of us now, every single one of us 'cause we haven't got the guts to do anything about it! And that's why I'm batterin' the Jesus outta' here soon as I gets a call before I ends up like the rest of ye!

JACK

Ya brazen little pup, I wish I could get a swipe at ya!

UNCLE PETER

He's right…

LEO

'Cause we're locked in, now they can do what they want with us and one thing I can tell ya for sure after bein' up there for the last fifteen years, the rest of Canada don't give a shit if they drowned the lot of us! But that's it, that's the way it goes. And as far as rural Newfoundland goes, there's not the hell of a lot in Gander, Corner Brook, St. John's, or even Clarenville give a shit either!

UNCLE PETER

All them years down a mine shaft haven't done him one bit of harm I can tell ya that…

Scene 3

Mary is sitting at the table reading from an old folder when Leo comes in the door.

MARY

That was a fine haul of lobsters you and Vince got this mornin'.

LEO

Not bad…What are ya readin'?

MARY

Some old papers I dug out.

Leo looks over her shoulder.

MARY

Some of the old papers from '49 that the Responsible crowd were sendin' around.

LEO

Bullshit is all it was then…same as now.

MARY

Pretty interestin' stuff to look at fifty years later…see here where it got all these points laid out…under Confederation we should in all probability lose our market in Europe for salt cod…

Bill and the ghost of Uncle Peter come in the door and go over to see what's being read.

BILL

We did…

MARY

'Under Confederation Canadians could invade our fishing grounds'…

BILL

They did and licensed the Europeans and the Japanese to do the same…

MARY

'Under Confederation our fisheries would drop back to the conditions of generations ago'…

BILL

They have…in 1949 we had about sixty-five percent of the salt fish trade in the world…sixty-five percent! We now got less than half a percent!

LEO

Oh Christ, will youse two give it up…

BILL

Listen here, you got your call, you're goin' back up there, ya got yer job back…Canada has been good to you like ya said…but it hasn't been good to all of us God damn it!

LEO

Why would the Canadian government let all that go to rat shit! Ya goes on about it all the time like ya knows every God damn answer to everything, but why in the name of Christ would they do that to us...like they had it all planned out!

UNCLE PETER

Aha! There it is, they did, the calculating bastards! Wheat my son...Western Canadian wheat is what started it. They would trade off our fish for wheat exports and they kept tradin' off for just about anything else they wanted a hand in, whether it were Europe, Russia or Japan...here give 'em more fish...they had the God damn nerve to tell us no more quotas for this, no more quotas for that and then turn around and license another six foreign and Canadian draggers and trawlers. The only difference in Newfoundland and other places ya hear about, Leo, my son, is that they're not shootin' us...

BILL

Not yet they're not, Uncle Peter...not yet.

LEO

What...?

BILL

Nothin', my son...I was just thinkin' about Christmas that's all.

LEO

Ah fer' Christ, what are ya on about, Dad...this is only June b'y.

BILL

Christmas is a long way away, isn't it?

Uncle Peter and Bill look at each other for the first time.

Scene 4

Bill is laying on the small daybed in the kitchen where Uncle Peter and Jack stand over him. Sarah and Mary sit at the table.

MARY

He's not very good, girl…there's nothin' they can do.

SARAH

He certainly knows, doesn't he.

MARY

He knows, and he's ready…I hope I'm as ready when my time comes.

SARAH

Stop it, Mary…where's Vince?

MARY

Bill was on about Christmas again when I went upstairs and when I come down, Vince was gone and Bill were asleep so I don't know where he's to, girl.

SARAH

And no word from poor Leo?

MARY

I got no way to get hold of 'im…it breaks my heart, it do. Last time he called, he and 'is Father got into another racket and I didn't even

Des Walsh

get a chance to ask 'im where he was to, so I don't know when I'm likely to hear word from 'im.

Pause.

SARAH

What about the time in the school next Friday night, this Soiree '99 thing to go along with Canada Day?

MARY

No…I told ya before, even if Bill were up and around, I'm not liftin' a finger for it and neither is Vince. All they ever sends out is a box of Canadian flags and we're s'posed to go down on the wharf and wave 'em around like a crowd of fools…besides, July 1st is Memorial Day, not Canada Day.

UNCLE PETER

Give it to 'er Mary.

JACK

She don't mean no harm Uncle Peter.

UNCLE PETER

Canada Day…sweet Jesus and all that's good and holy. July 1st is Memorial Day when us poor Newfoundlanders got slaughtered. Just imagine if they tried to make Canada Day on Jean Baptiste Day in Quebec…no sir, they would've changed Canada Day, but not here. No one asked us if we wanted our own national holiday thrown out with the dishwater…July 1st it is, they said and the hells flames with Newfoundland, and now there's this Soiree '99 bullshit for the fiftieth anniversary…they'll probably have booths set up sellin' square rollin' pins and cans of fog! Lord sweet merciful Christ, put a fiddle player on a telephone book and everything is s'posed to be all right from Cape Chidley to Bonavista!

SARAH

It's just they called out to me from Ottawa and they…

MARY

Called ya from Ottawa…that sets you right in a tizzy, don't it, Sarah, that they called ya from Ottawa. Well, Ottawa didn't call ya when they laid ya off from the post office did they. Ya gets a miserable call from some little snot-nosed fella' in Halifax sayin' they're restructurin' Canada Post so as to serve us better and now we gotta' drive across the bay to send a letter.

SARAH

Forget it, Mary…forget I asked.

BILL

I wish I kept the newspapers…

MARY

What's that, Bill?

BILL

Remember how we'd always see somethin' in the paper, somethin' that'd make me blood boil…like the time they were goin' across coast to coast gettin' everyone's say on the state of the country's finances…

UNCLE PETER

That's right, they were goin' out to the people they said.

BILL

And they only come as far as Halifax and they asked 'em why they weren't comin' to Newfoundland and they said because they thought it would be a waste of the Committee's time, they'd hear nothin' new they said…

MARY

Yes, honey, I remember that…

UNCLE PETER

And what about the time that frigger in Calgary or somewhere out there said that there were too many immigrants and Newfoundlanders showin' up on his doorstep…

BILL

If I had kept all them articles you'd have some pile of stuff in a box.

SARAH

For what, Bill, what good would it do?

BILL

To put it in a book or somethin', God damn it, so people would know the truth of it…that's the one clear problem for us is that we forgets everything too quick….

JACK

'Cause we're too busy tryin' to feed ourselves is why.

UNCLE PETER

And they God damn well knows that too, Jack, my son. That's the way to get a crowd to stay curled up in the corner with not a peep out of 'em…keep 'em hungry and keep 'em poor.

SARAH

Good Lord when you crowd passes on you'll be the last of 'em for sure.

MARY

And what then, Sarah, you tell me that…what then?

The door opens and Vince walks in with a spruce tree.

SARAH

What in the Lord…?

VINCE

Here she is then, Dad…you said how much ya loved Christmas and a Christmas tree.

JACK

There's a laddio for ya now I know.

VINCE

Where's the box with all the stuff in it, Mom?

BILL

By God she's a dandy tree, my son.

Mary goes offstage.

SARAH

It's the end of June!

UNCLE PETER

Who cares, Sarah?

JACK

The man wanted a tree…he gotta' tree.

BILL

Did ya go in behind the Nap like I told ya.

VINCE

She was right where you'd said she'd be.

Mary comes back with a box, lays it on the table and begins removing lights and Christmas decorations.

SARAH

You crowd have slipped right off the edge of the wharf this time for sure…

BILL

I seen that tree winter before last and I knew she'd be a dandy.

UNCLE PETER

There's not a lot of time, Bill…

BILL

I know, Uncle Peter…

SARAH

There he goes again…when did that start, Mary?

MARY

With Uncle Peter…oh I don't know, a couple of months ago…

BILL

Just imagine Newfoundlanders dying away from home and being buried there, that gotta' be the saddest thing in the world…will Leo ever come home again I wonder?

VINCE

Never mind that now, Dad…Leo can look out himself. Don't get vexed over it, ya needs to rest is all…

UNCLE PETER

It's all right, Vince, let 'em go…

BILL

Mary…

MARY

Yes, sweetheart…

BILL

Come sit closer will ya…Sarah, you do the tree will ya?

Mary sits closer to Bill while Sarah continues decorating the tree.

JACK

I'm not sure that's such a good idea, Bill, Sarah was never much with a Christmas tree.

BILL

She'll do fine, Jack…

SARAH

Oh God, don't start on Jack now, that gives me the shivers.

BILL

You gonna be able to look out to everything, Mary.

MARY

Sure I'll be grand. They're liable to open the fishery any day at all and there'll be more cod hauled in over the rails than has been seen along this coast for years.

BILL

And it's not just money, is it, Vince...

VINCE

No it's not, Dad...

BILL

Get a hold of Leo, Mary, do ya hear me, ya knows I loves 'im and wants only what's best for 'im...tell 'im that.

MARY

I will, sweetheart....ya knows I will.

BILL

Don't die in a foreign country, Vince, my son, and mark my words, Canada is a foreign country to us crowd...there's some would like to see every one out of this place and have it be left for gulls and tourists, but don't let 'em do it, do ya hear me, Vince?

VINCE

I hear ya...

UNCLE PETER

Funny thing about watching a man or a woman die is that we all want to make sure somethin' is left…most of us anyway.

JACK

He was always a heartbroken man…

BILL

God damn ya, Jack I never got over it b'y that's all there's to it…'49 was one thing but the last going off, how we been treated the last ten to fifteen years or so have been the worst of it…but that's enough now, I don't think I got much more to say…

UNCLE PETER

He's comin' Jack…

JACK

You get 'em on the other side there, Uncle Peter.

Jack and Uncle Peter move closer to Bill on the day bed.

BILL

The song, Mary…the Christmas one…

MARY

What, honey?

BILL

The Green's Harbour Carol…sing it will ya, my love?

MARY

The moon shines bright and the stars give light
A little before it is day

Des Walsh

The moon shines bright and the stars give light
A little before it is day
Our Lord our God he calls on us
And bids us to watch and to pray.

Awake, awake good people all,
Awake and ye shall hear
Awake, awake good people all,
Awake and ye shall hear
Our Lord our God died on the cross
For those whom he loved so dear.

BILL

You too, Vince…come on, Sarah.

Vince and Sarah join in.

MARY, VINCE AND SARAH *(in unison)*

There's a talent at your head, young man
And another at your feet
There's a talent at your head, young man
And another at your feet
When your good deeds and your bad ones
Together they both shall meet.

BILL

Get in there, Uncle Peter…Jack…

ALL CHARACTERS *(in unison)*

Farewell, farewell Jerusalem,
When shall I come to thee?
Farewell, farewell Jerusalem,

The Moon Shone Bright

When shall I come to thee?
When all our troubles are at an end
Thy joys we soon shall see.

Uncle Peter and Jack help Bill up off the daybed and lead him him off to the side while the others continue singing.

My carol is done and I must be gone
I can stay no longer here
My carol is done and I must be gone
I can stay no longer here
God bless ye all both great and small
And send you a happy new year.

Mary, Vince and Sarah look down on the empty daybed.

MARY

Bill…Bill…goodnight sweet man.

VINCE

It'll come around, Dad…

UNCLE PETER

I don't know if there's enough spark left in the place, Vince.

MARY

Oh there's plenty of life left in 'er yet, Uncle Peter, plenty of life yet.